HAL•LEONARD
HARMONICA
PLAY•ALONG

ROCK HITS

CONTENTS

Harmonica by Clint Hoover

ISBN 978-1-4234-2326-3

Visit Hal Leonard Online at
www.halleonard.com

HAL•LEONARD®
CORPORATION
7777 W. BLUEMOUND RD. P.O. BOX 13819
MILWAUKEE, WISCONSIN 53213

Hand in My Pocket

Lyrics by Alanis Morissette
Music by Alanis Morissette and Glen Ballard

HARMONICA
Player: Alanis Morissette
Harp Key: G Diatonic

Intro
Moderate Rock ♩ = 92
G5
(Guitar & drums)

3

1. I'm

% Verse

G5

broke but I'm ___ hap-py, _____ I'm poor but I'm kind, _____ I'm

3. *See additional lyrics*

short but I'm ___ health - y, yeah. _____ I'm ___

high but I'm ground - ed, _____ I'm sane but I'm o - ver - whelmed, I'm

To Coda ⊕

lost but I'm hope - ful, ba - by. ___ And what it all comes down ___

Chorus

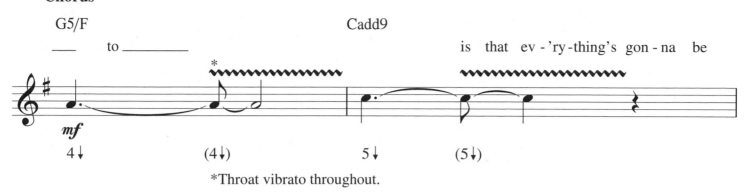

*Throat vibrato throughout.

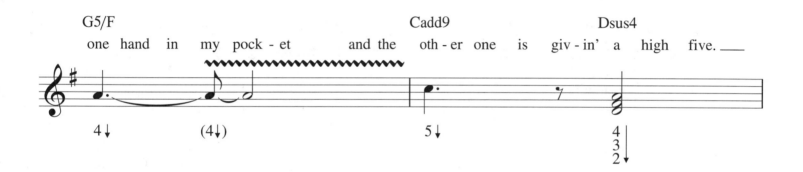

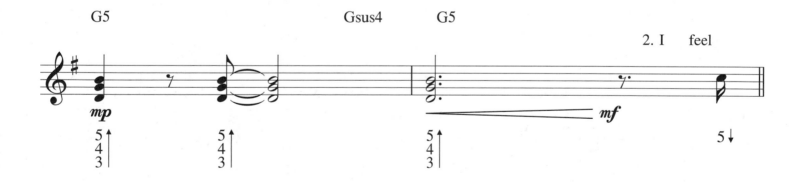

Verse

tired but I'm __ work - in', yeah. ___

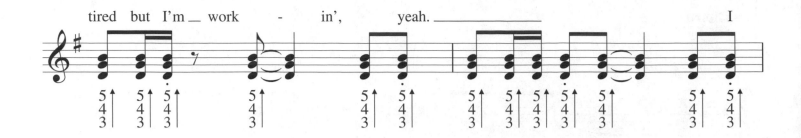

care but I'm __ rest - less, I'm here but I'm __ real - ly __ gone. I'm __

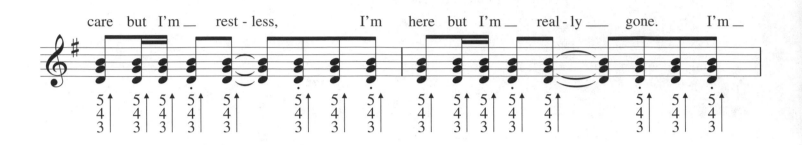

wrong and I'm __ sor - ry, ba - by. __ And what it all comes down __

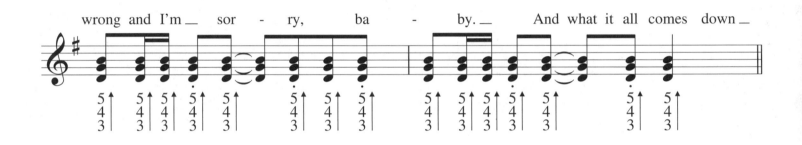

Chorus

G5/F   Cadd9

__ to _____   is that ev -'ry-thing's gon - na be

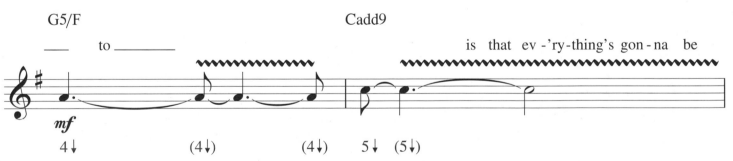

G5

quite al - right, _____   'cause I've __ got

G5

out just ___ yet, ___ 'cause I've _ got

G5/F   Cadd9   Dsus4

one hand in my __ pock-et   and the oth-er one is giv-in' a peace _ sign. __

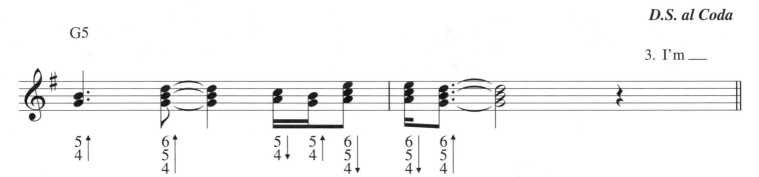

D.S. al Coda

G5

3. I'm ___

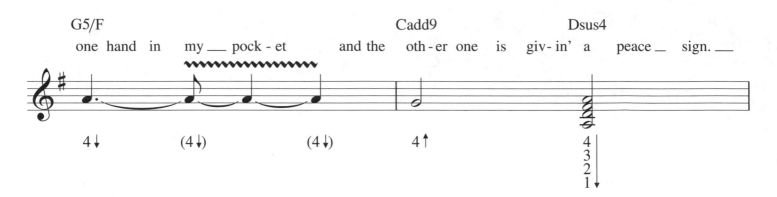

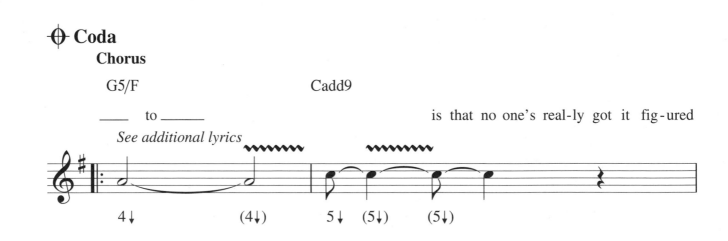

⊕ **Coda**

Chorus

G5/F   Cadd9

___ to _____   is that no one's real-ly got it fig-ured

See additional lyrics

G5

out just yet, _____   but I've _ got

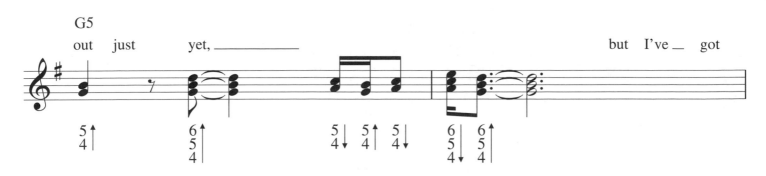

6

Additional Lyrics

3. I'm free but I'm focused,
   I'm green but I'm wise,
   I'm hard but I'm friendly, baby.
   I'm sad but I'm laughing,
   I'm brave but I'm chicken-shit,
   I'm sick but I'm pretty, baby.

Chorus And what it all comes down to, my friends, yeah,
   Is that everything's just fine, fine, fine,
   'Cause I've got one hand in my pocket
   And the other one is hailing a taxi-cab.

Karma Chameleon

Words and Music by George O'Dowd, Jon Moss,
Michael Craig, Roy Hay and Phil Pickett

HARMONICA
Player: Judd Lander
Harp Key: E♭ Diatonic

Intro

Moderately fast ♩ = 184

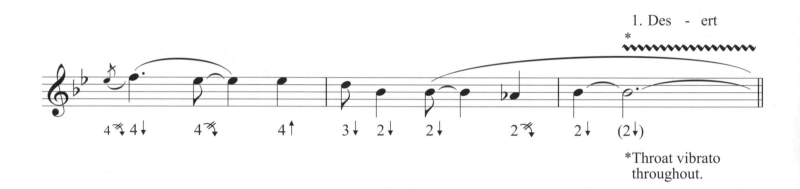

*Throat vibrato
throughout.

Verse

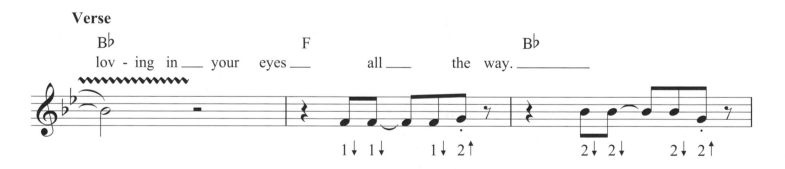

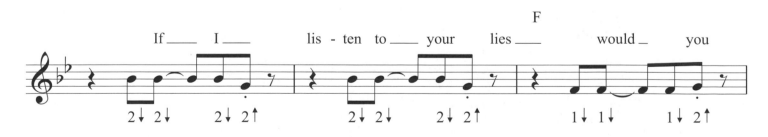

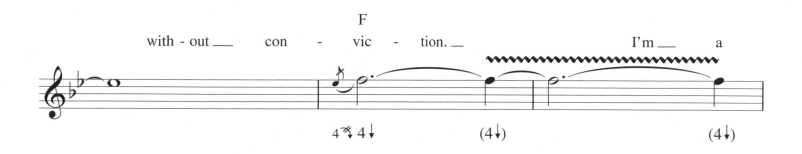

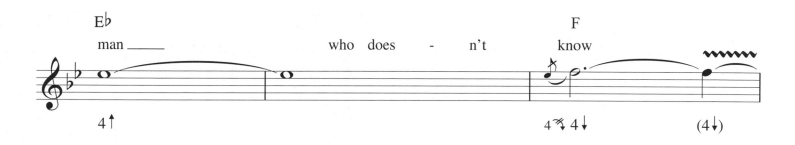

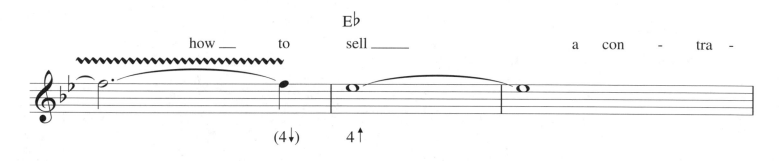

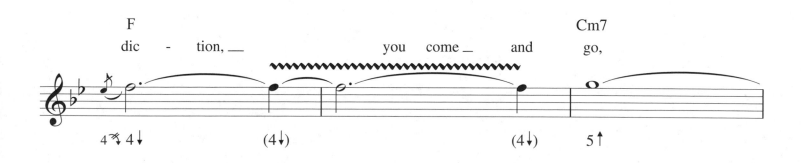

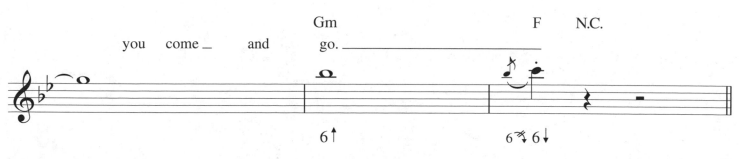

Chorus

Bb   F/A   Gm7

Kar-ma kar-ma kar-ma kar-ma   kar-ma cha-me - le - on,

1↓ 2↑ 3↑

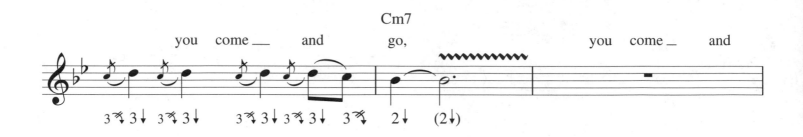

     Cm7

you come __ and   go,   you come __ and

3⤨3↓ 3⤨3↓   3⤨3↓3⤨3↓ 3⤨ 2↓   (2↓)

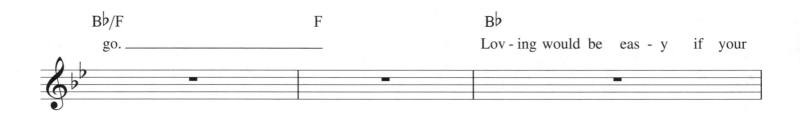

Bb/F   F   Bb

go. _____   Lov-ing would be eas - y   if your

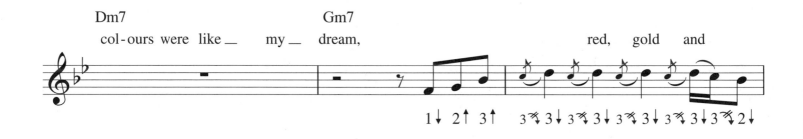

Dm7   Gm7

col-ours were like __ my __ dream,   red, gold and

1↓ 2↑ 3↑   3⤨3↓ 3⤨3↓ 3⤨3↓ 3⤨3↓3⤨2↓

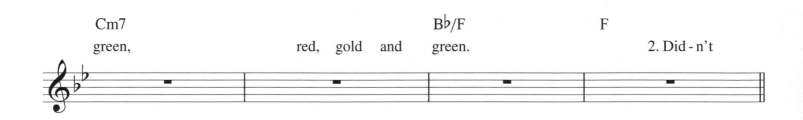

Cm7   Bb/F   F

green,   red, gold and green.   2. Did-n't

𝄋 **Verse**

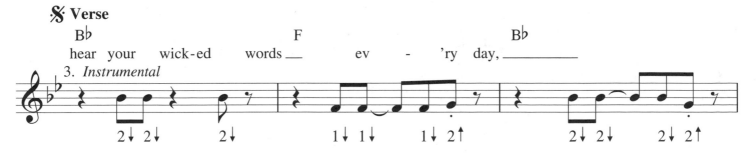

Bb   F   Bb

hear your wick-ed words __ ev - 'ry day, _____

3. *Instrumental*

2↓ 2↓   2↓   1↓ 1↓   1↓ 2↑   2↓ 2↓   2↓ 2↑

and __ you __ used to be __ so sweet __ I heard __ you

F

2↓ 2↓   2↓ 2↑   2↓ 2↓   2↓ 2↑   1↓ 1↓   1↓ 2↑

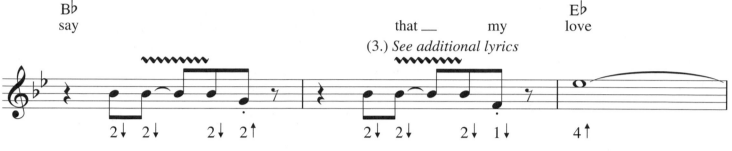

Bb
say   that __   my   love

Eb

(3.) *See additional lyrics*

2↓ 2↓   2↓ 2↑   2↓ 2↓   2↓ 1↓   4↑

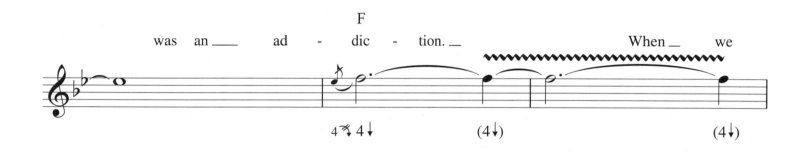

was an __ ad - dic - tion. __   When __ we

F

4⤥ 4↓   (4↓)   (4↓)

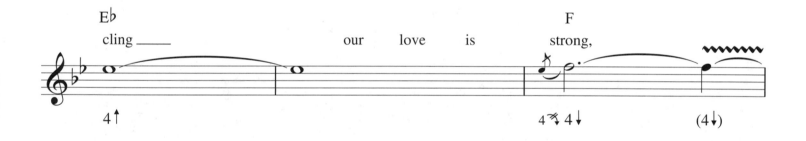

Eb
cling ____   our love is

F
strong,

4↑   4⤥ 4↓   (4↓)

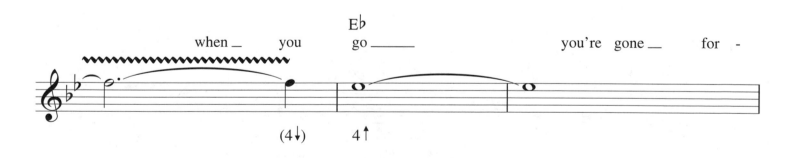

when __ you   go ____   you're gone __   for -

Eb

(4↓)   4↑

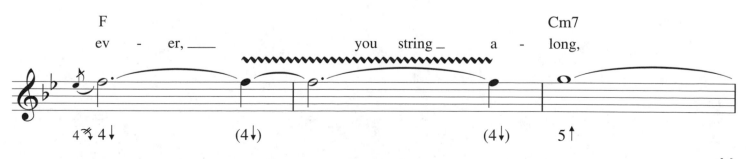

F
ev - er, ____   you string __ a - long,

Cm7

4⤥ 4↓   (4↓)   (4↓)   5↑

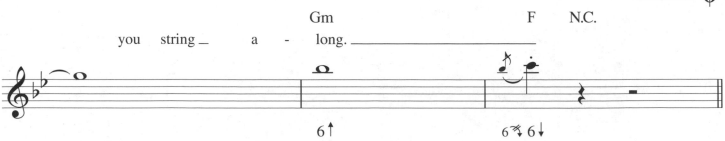

Chorus

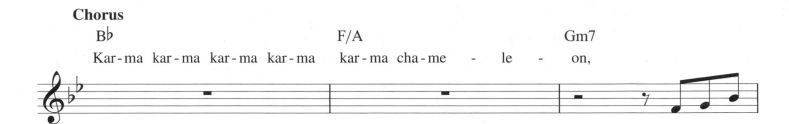

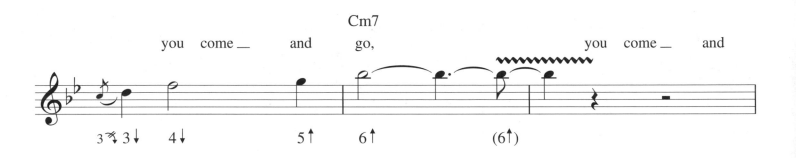

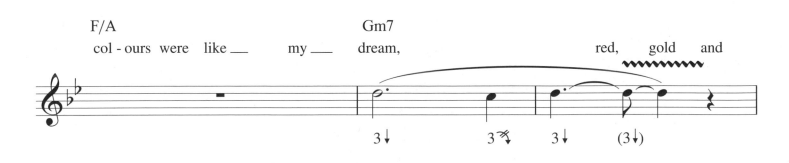

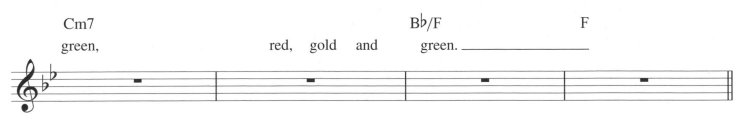

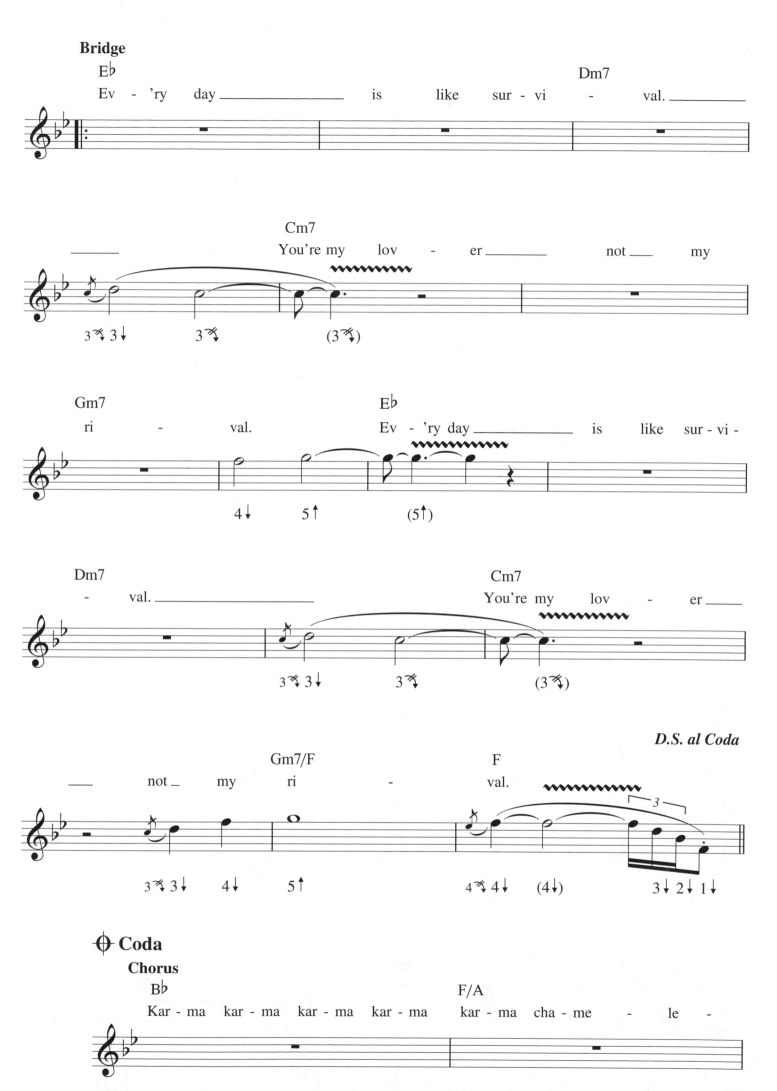

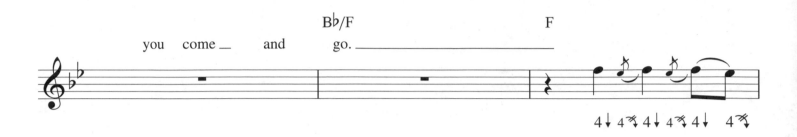

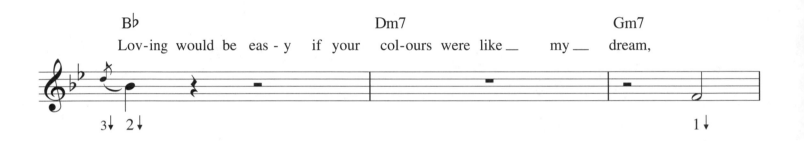

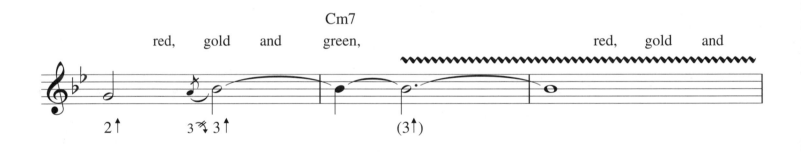

Half-time feel

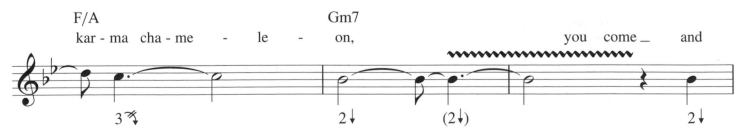

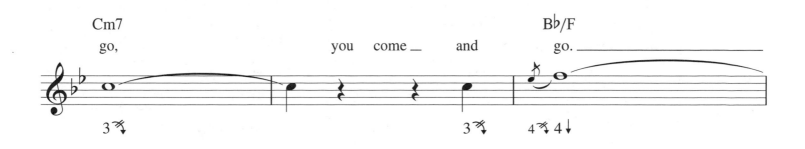

go, you come ___ and go. _____ **Bb/F**

Cm7

3 ↘ 3 ↘ 4 ↘ 4 ↓

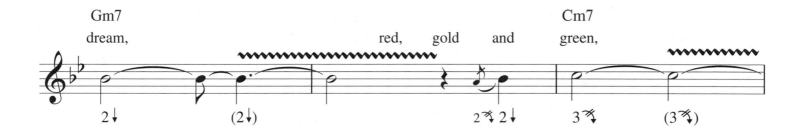

F ___ **Bb** Lov-ing would be eas - y if your col-ours were like ___ my ___ **Dm7**

(4↓) 3↘ 3↓ 3↘ (3↘)

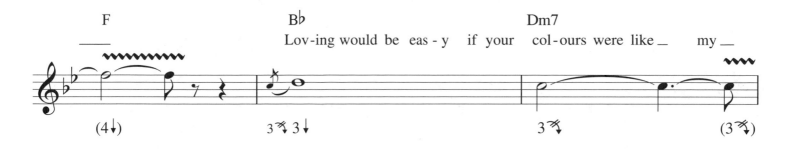

Gm7 dream, red, gold and green, **Cm7**

2↓ (2↓) 2↘ 2↓ 3↘ (3↘)

End half-time feel

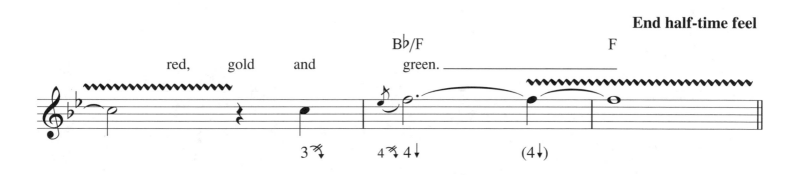

red, gold and green. _____ **Bb/F** **F**

3↘ 4↘ 4↓ (4↓)

Outro-Chorus

Bb Kar - ma kar - ma kar - ma kar - ma kar - ma cha - me - le - **F/A**

Gm7 on, you come ___ and go, **Cm7**

1↓ 2↑ 3↑ 3↘ 3↓ 3↘ 3↓ 3↘ 3↓ 3↘ 3↓ 3↘ 3↑

you come __ and go. __

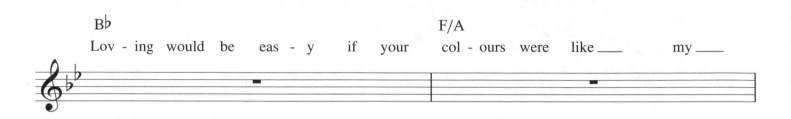

Lov - ing would be eas - y if your col - ours were like ___ my ___

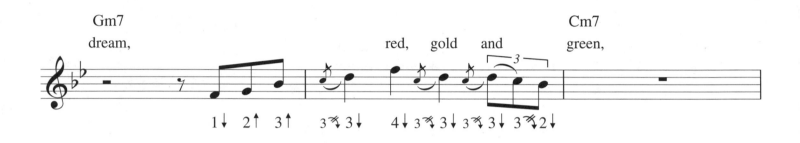

dream, red, gold and green,

red, gold and green. __

Kar - ma kar - ma kar - ma kar - ma kar - ma cha - me - le - on,

you come __ and go, you come __ and

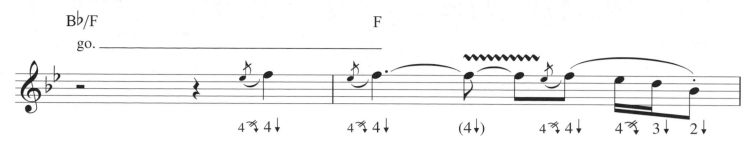

Bb/F   F

go. _____

4✗ 4↓   4✗ 4↓   (4↓)   4✗ 4↓   4✗ 3↓   2↓

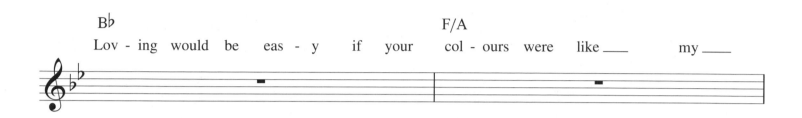

Bb   F/A

Lov - ing would be eas - y if your col - ours were like ___ my ___

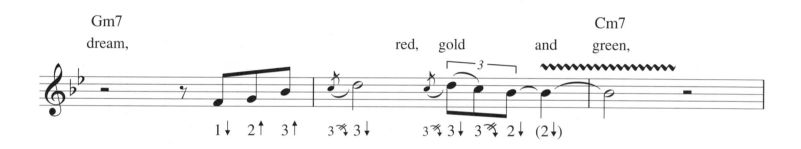

Gm7   Cm7

dream,   red, gold   and   green,

1↓   2↑   3↑   3✗ 3↓   3✗ 3↓ 3✗ 2↓ (2↓)

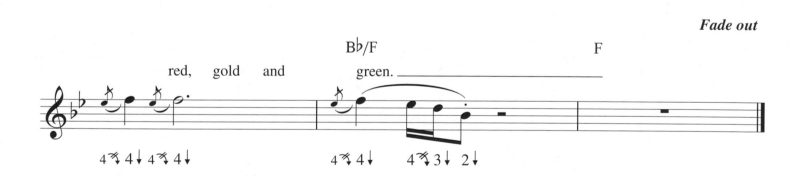

                     Bb/F   F

red, gold and   green. _____

4✗ 4↓ 4✗ 4↓   4✗ 4↓   4✗ 3↓ 2↓

Additional Lyrics

3. I'm a man without conviction.
    I'm a man who doesn't know
    How to sell a contradiction.
    You come and go,
    You come and go.

Middle of the Road

Words and Music by Chrissie Hynde

HARMONICA
Player: Chrissie Hynde
Harp Key: D Diatonic

Intro
Moderately fast ♩ = 168

N.C.
(Drums)

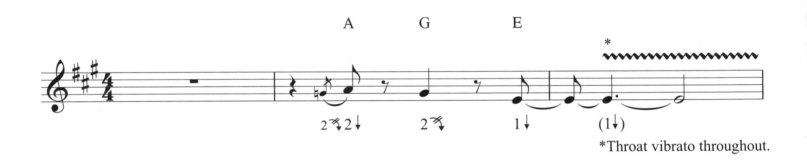

*Throat vibrato throughout.

Oo. _____

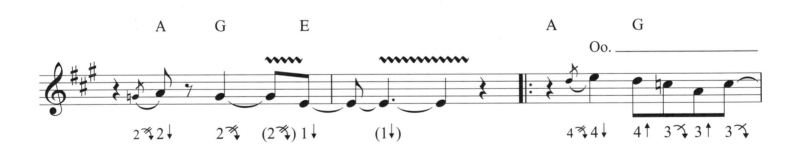

1., 2., 3.   4.   **Verse**

1. The mid-dle of the road _____

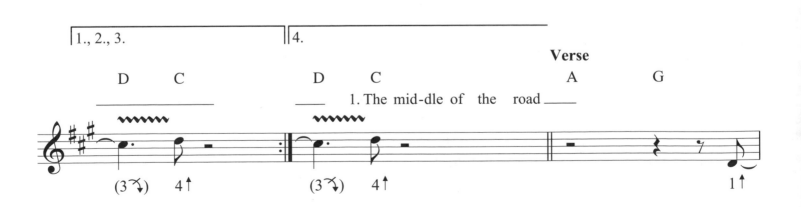

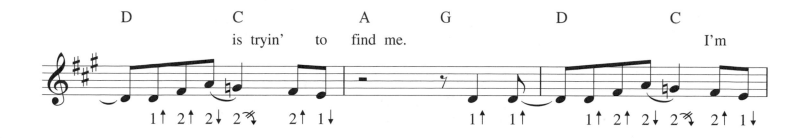

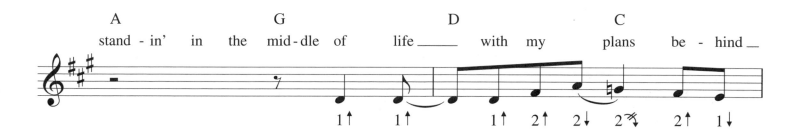

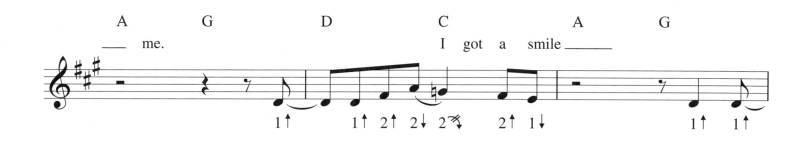

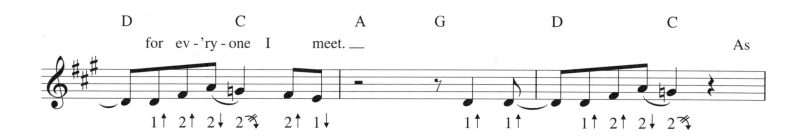

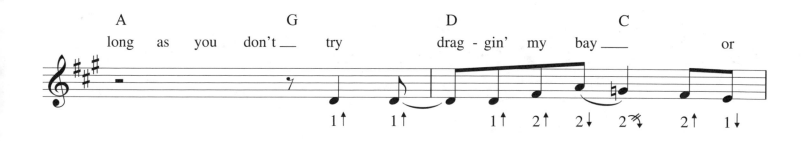

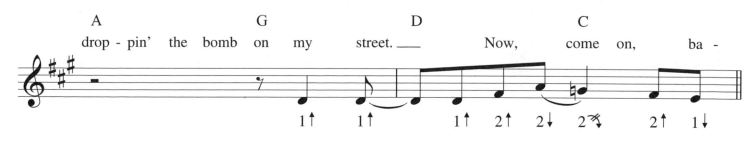

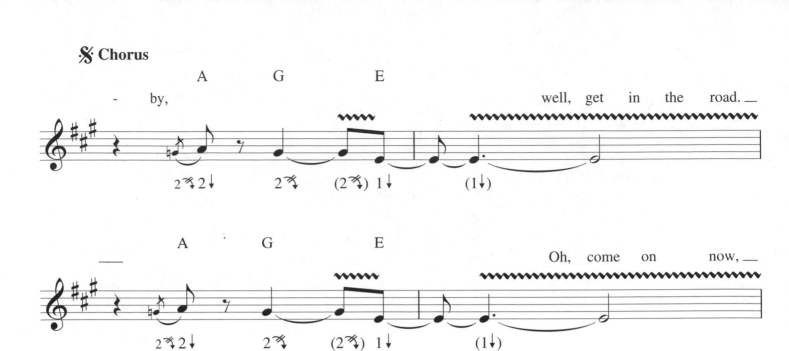

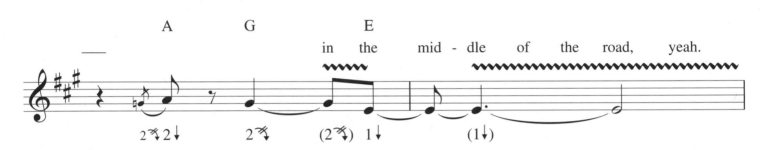

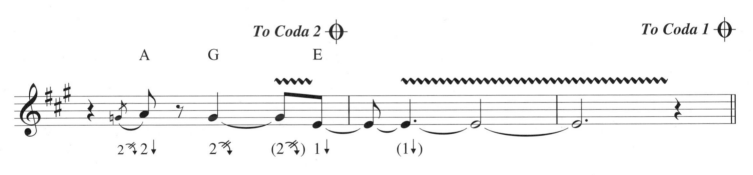

To Coda 2 ⊕   *To Coda 1* ⊕

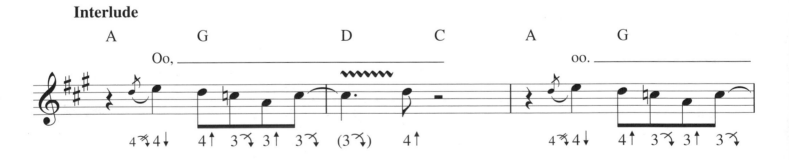

Interlude

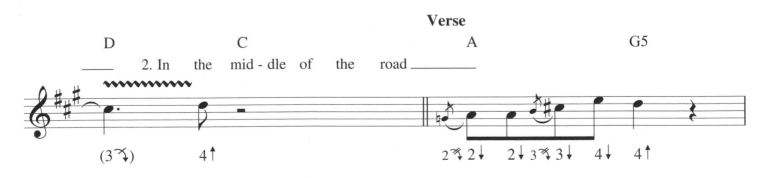

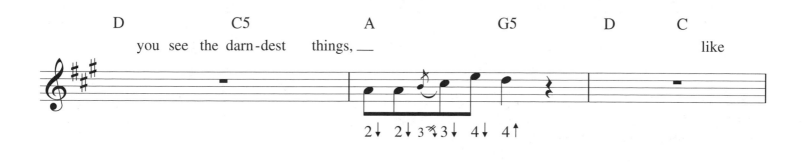

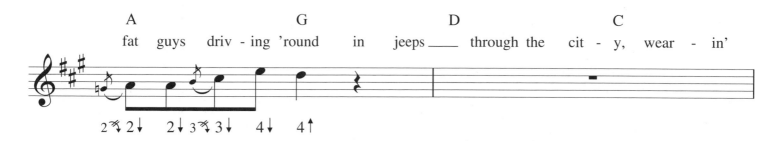

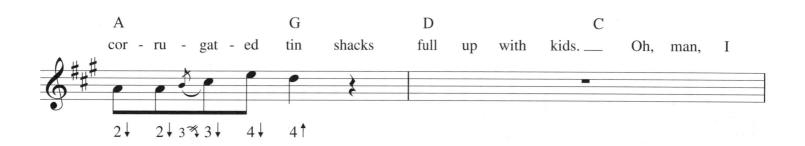

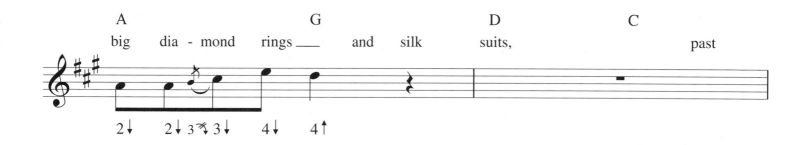

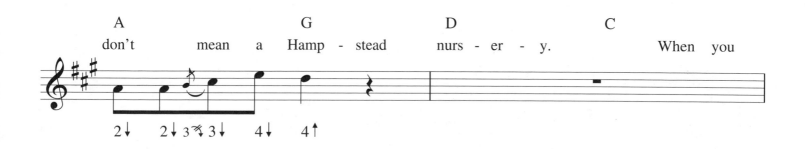

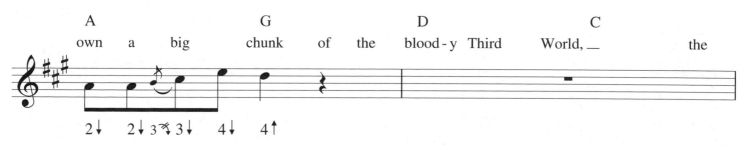

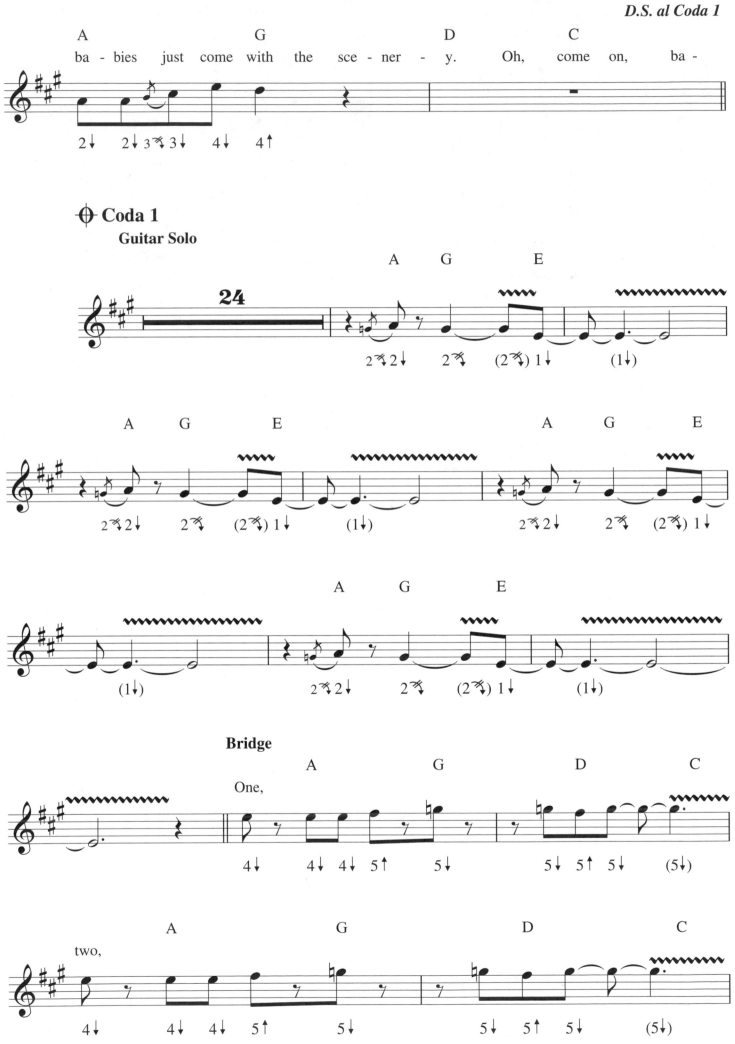

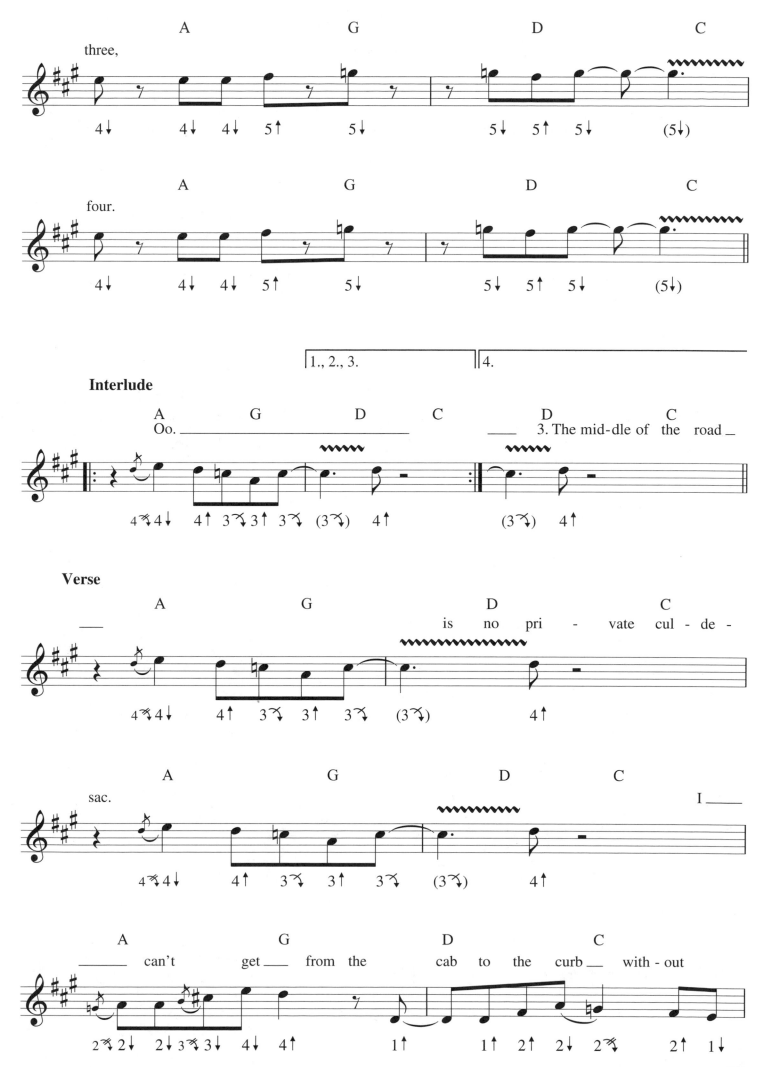

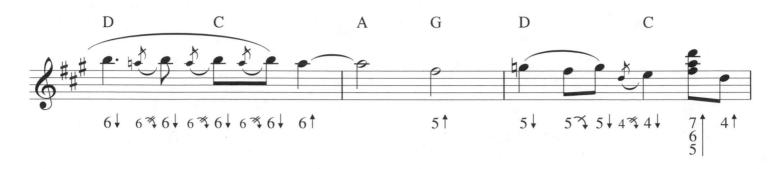

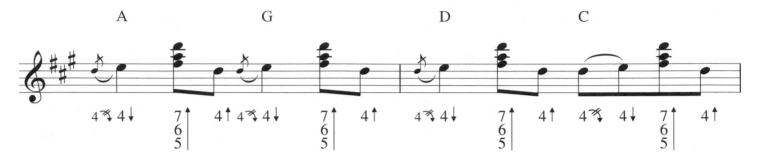

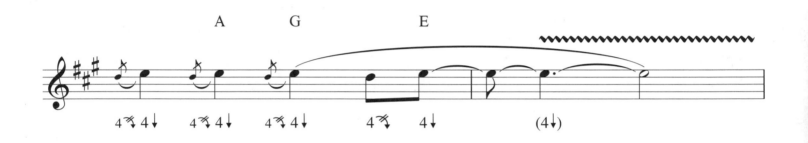

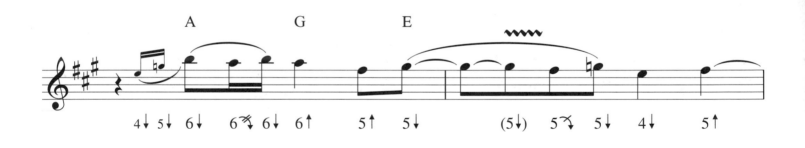

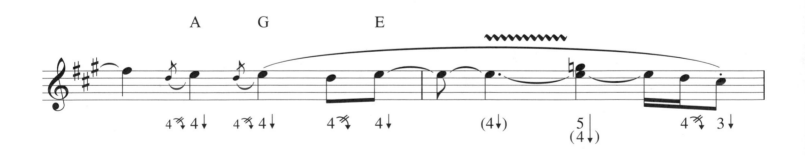

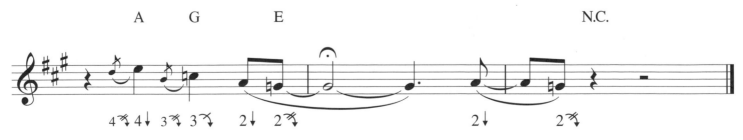

26

Rock Me

Words and Music by Alan Niven, Mark Kendall, Jack Russell and Michael Lardie

HARMONICA
Player: Michael Lardie
Harp Key: D Diatonic

Intro

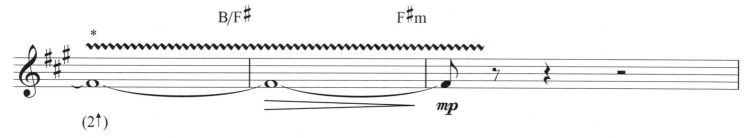

*Throat vibrato throughout.

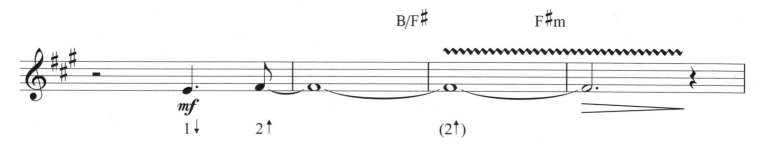

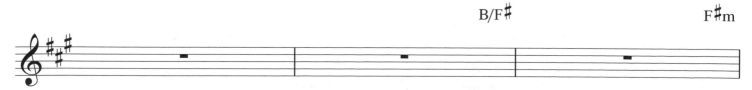

1↓ 2↓ 2↑   (2↑)

Verse

F#m

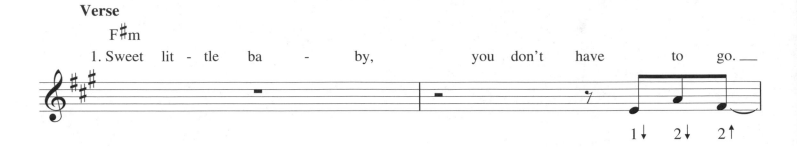

1. Sweet lit - tle ba - by, you don't have to go. ___

1↓ 2↓ 2↑

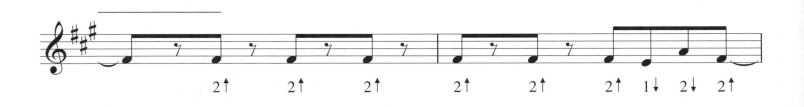

2↑ 2↑ 2↑ 2↑ 2↑ 2↑ 1↓ 2↓ 2↑

Lit - tle ba - by, tell me you won't go. ___

2↑ 2↑ 2↑ 2↑ 2↑ 2↑ 1↓ 2↓ 2↑

Oh,

2↑ 2↑ 2↑ 2↑ 2↑ 2↑ 1↓ 2↓ 2↑

we'd be so good to - geth - er if we ___ had the time. ___

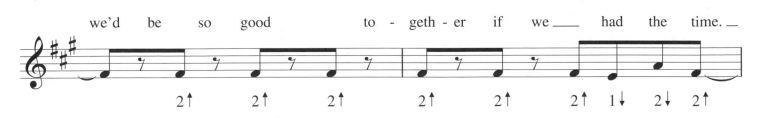

2↑ 2↑ 2↑ 2↑ 2↑ 2↑ 1↓ 2↓ 2↑

Pre-Chorus

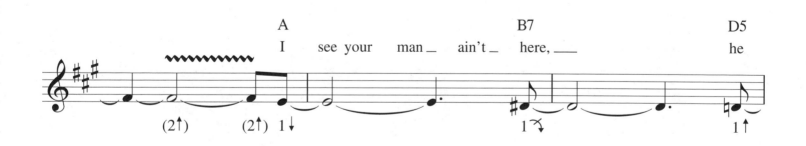

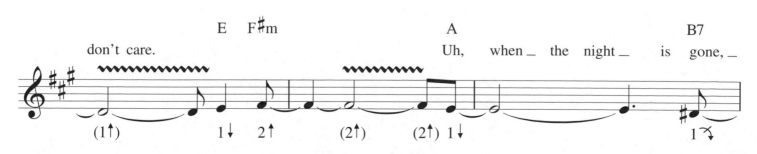

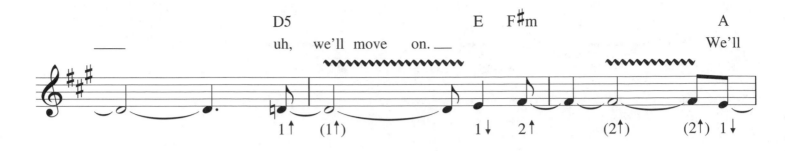

D5   E   F♯m   A

uh, we'll move on. ___ We'll

B7   D5   E5

have to find ___ a way ___ to face ___ an-oth - er day. ___

Interlude

F♯m

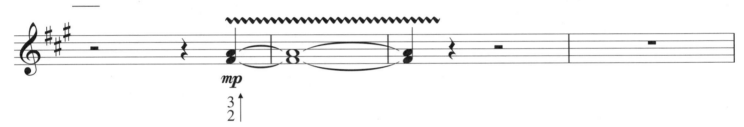

Verse

F♯m

2. Search the world ___ for some - one I'll nev -

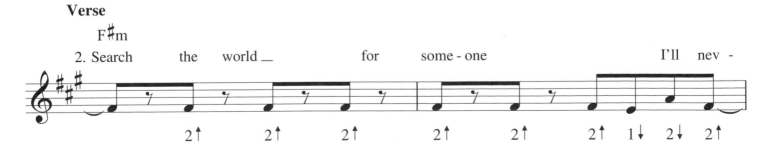

30

er find. __

Some - one who ain't, __   oo, _____   the __ hurt - in' _____

__ kind. __

Pre-Chorus

F#m   A   B7   D5

Oo, _____   if you   stay __   the   night, __   oh, __   yeah. __

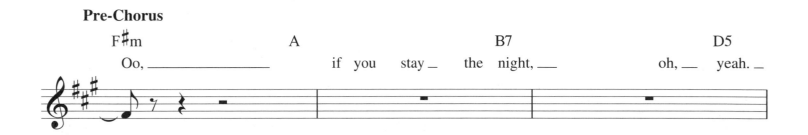

E   F#m   A   B7

We'll make the   wrong __ seem   right, __

𝄊 **Chorus**

D5   E5   F#5   C#5 D5

so   come on   now. __ _____ Rock _____ me,   rock __

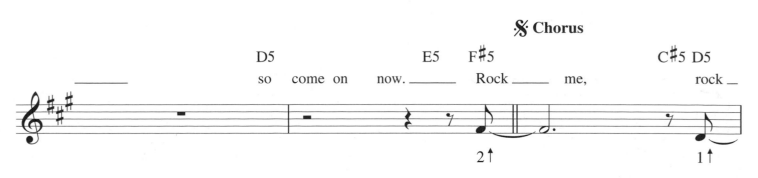

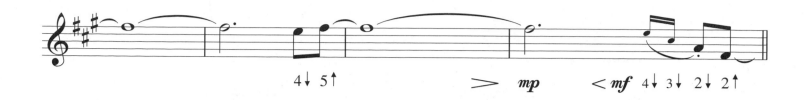

4↓ 5↑   >   *mp*   < *mf* 4↓ 3↓ 2↓ 2↑

Verse

F#m

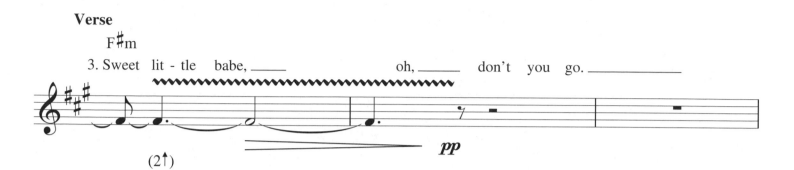

3. Sweet lit - tle babe, _____ oh, _____ don't you go. _____

(2↑)   *pp*

You __ ain't so, __ oo, _____ in - no - cent I _____ know. __

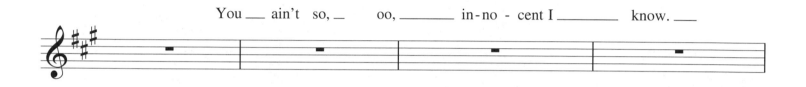

Pre-Chorus

F#m   A   B7

Oo, _____ I know your heart's _ like mine, _

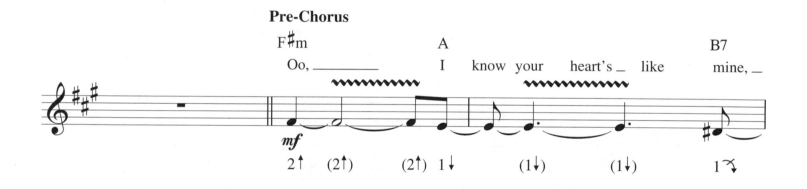

2↑ (2↑) (2↑) 1↓ (1↓) (1↓) 1↷

D5   E   F#m   A

_____ oh, __ yeah. _____ And

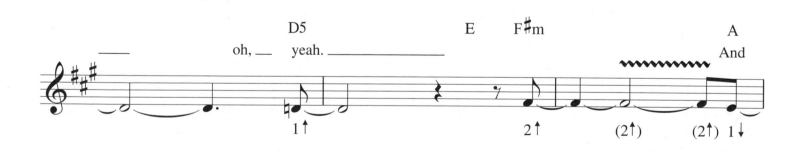

1↑   2↑ (2↑) (2↑) 1↓

B7   D5   E   F#m

I will find _ the time _____ to make you _ mine. __ Oo, _

(1↓) (1↓) 1↷   1↑ (1↑)   2↑

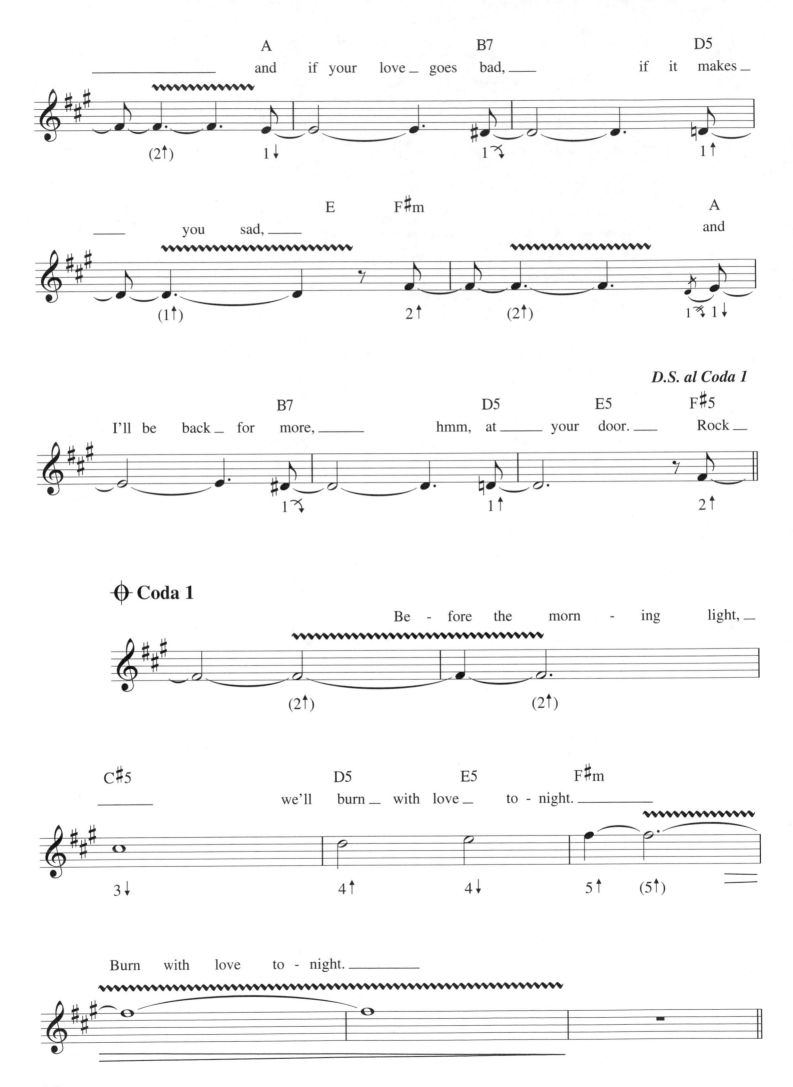

Guitar Solo

F#m　　　　　　　　　　　　　B7　　　　　　　D5
And when your man ___ don't care, ___　　I will ___

E　F#m　　　　　　　　　A　　　　　　　　B7
___　be there. ___　　You still be - long ___ in real ___

D.S. al Coda 2

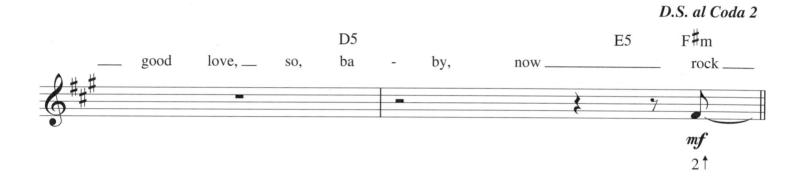

D5　　　　　　　　　　　　　E5　F#m
___ good love, ___ so, ba - by,　now _____ rock ____

mf
2↑

⊕ **Coda 2**

There's　no　wrong ___　or　right, ___

(2↑)

Chorus

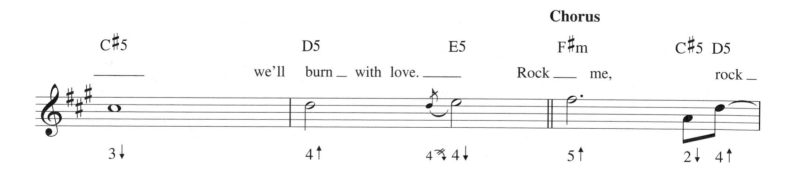

C#5　　　　　D5　　　　　E5　　　　F#m　　　　C#5 D5
___　we'll burn ___ with love. _____　Rock ___ me,　rock ___

3↓　　　　　4↑　　　4✕4↓　　　5↑　　　2↓ 4↑

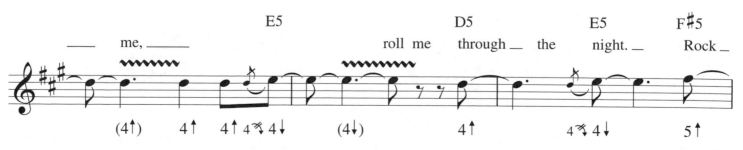

E5　　　　　　　　　D5　　　　E5　　　F#5
___ me, _____　roll me through ___ the night. ___　Rock ___

(4↑)　4↑　4↑4✕4↓　(4↓)　4↑　4✕4↓　5↑

Outro-Guitar Solo

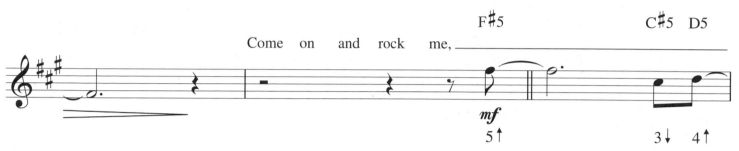

Come on and rock me, _____

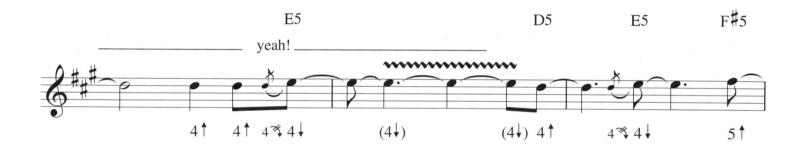

yeah! _____

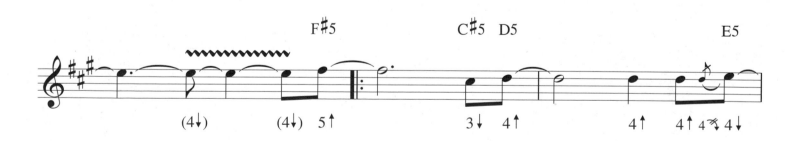

Repeat and fade

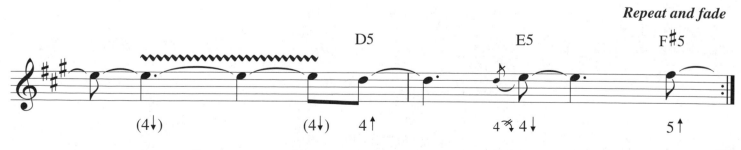

Small Town

Words and Music by John Mellencamp

HARMONICA
Player: Larry Crane
Harp Key: B Diatonic

*Throat vibrato throughout.

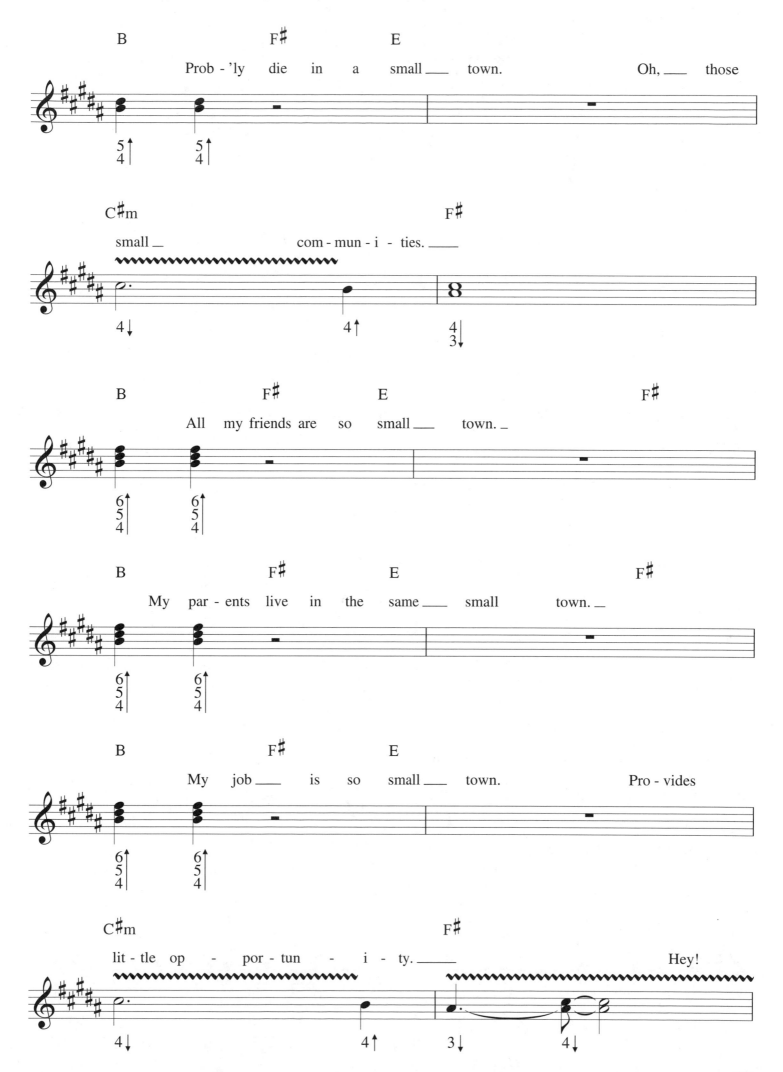

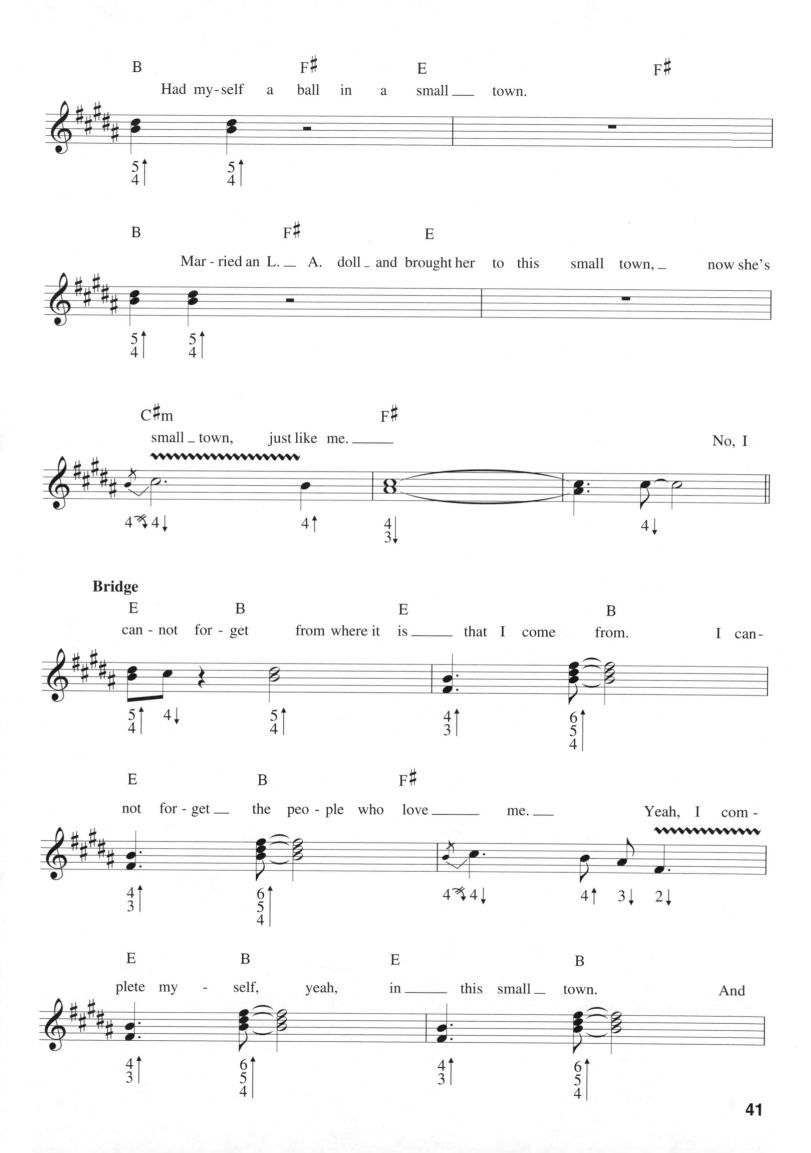

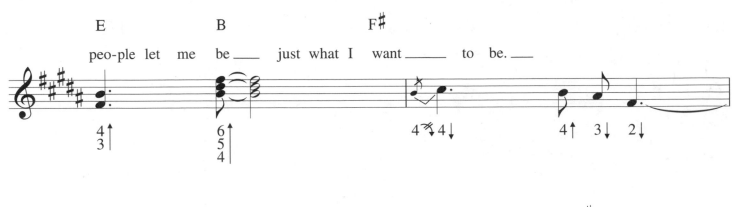

peo-ple let me be ____ just what I want ____ to be. ____

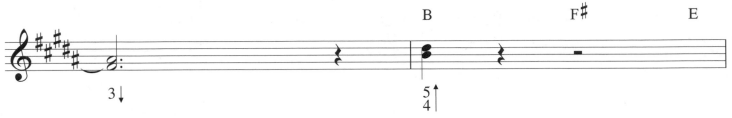

Ooh, ____ my, my, ____ my, yeah. ____ Ooh, yeah, yeah, yeah. ____

Interlude

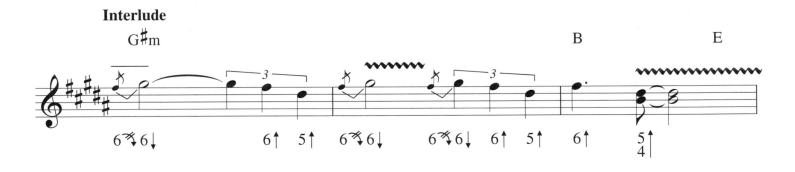

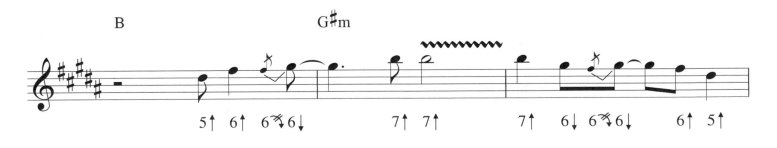

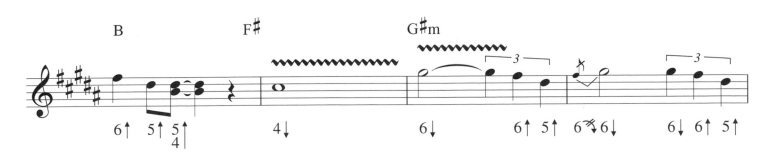

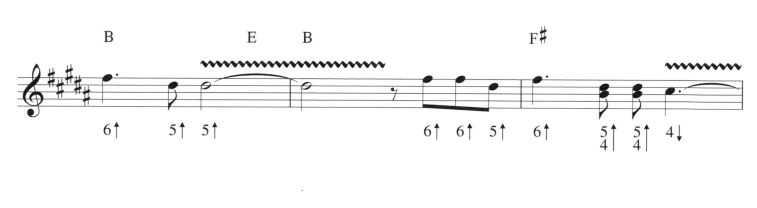

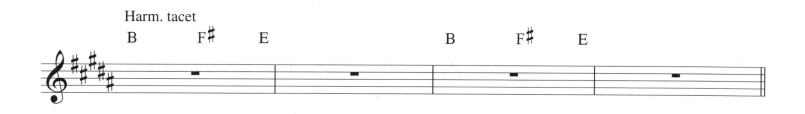

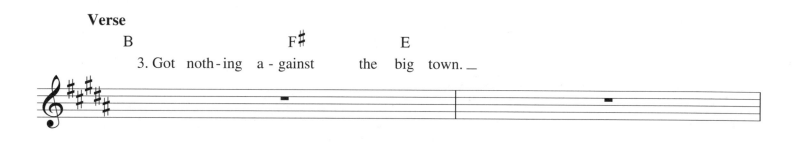

Verse

B   F# E

3. Got noth-ing a-gainst   the big town. __

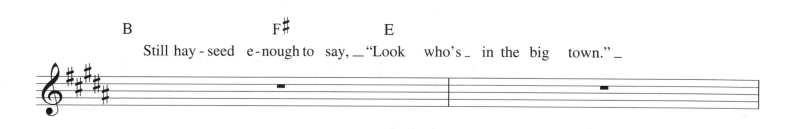

B   F# E

Still hay-seed e-nough to say, __ "Look   who's __ in the big   town." __

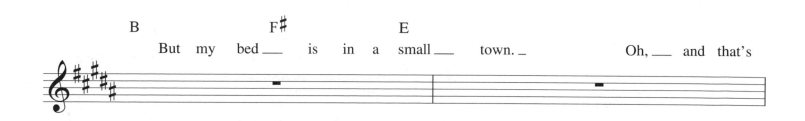

B   F# E

But my bed __ is in a small __ town. __   Oh, __ and that's

Smokin' in the Boys Room

Words and Music by Michael Koda and Michael Lutz

HARMONICA

Player: Vince Neil
Harp Key: C Diatonic

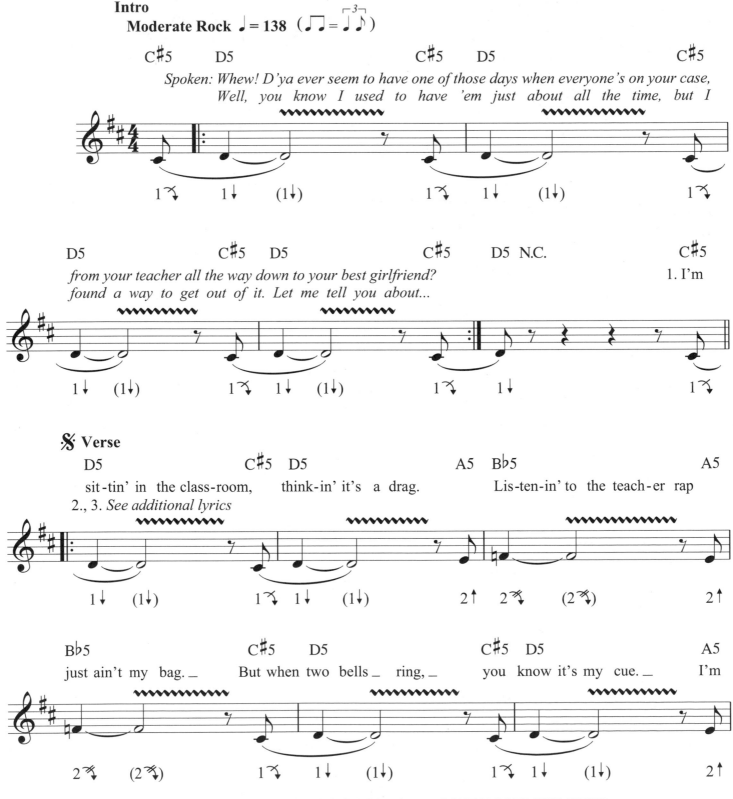

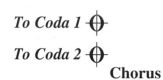

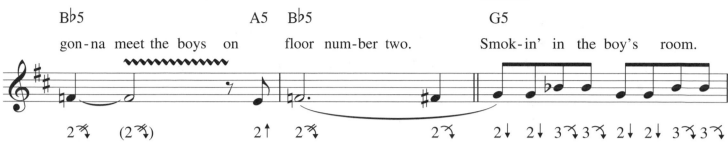

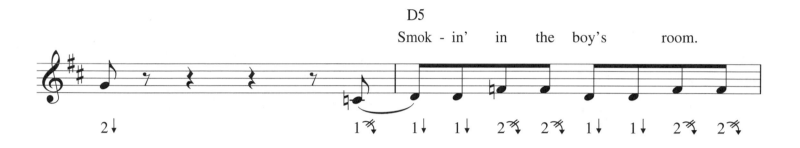

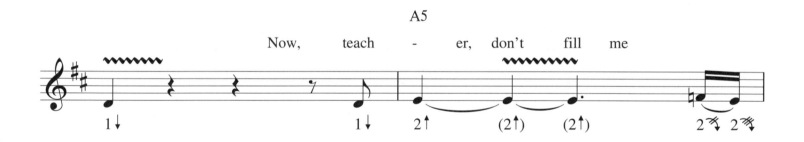

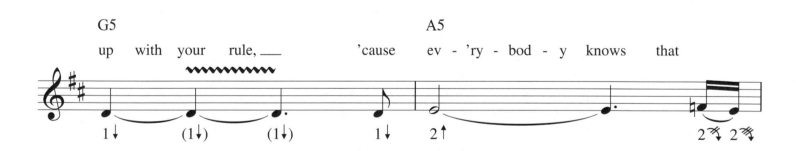

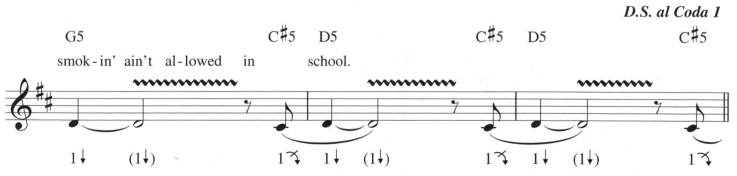

⊕ Coda 1

Chorus

G5

Smok - in' in the boy's room. I was

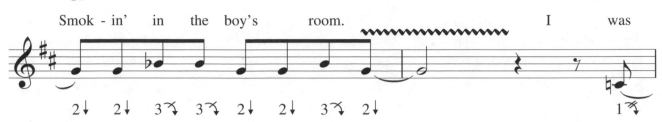

2↓ 2↓ 3↗ 3↗ 2↓ 2↓ 3↗ 2↓ 1↗

D5

smok - in' in the boy's room. Now, teach -

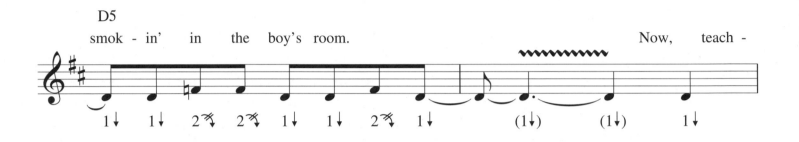

1↓ 1↓ 2↗ 2↗ 1↓ 1↓ 2↗ 1↓ (1↓) (1↓) 1↓

A5   G5

- er, don't fill me up with your rule, ___ 'cause

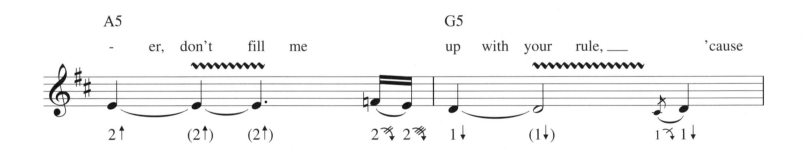

2↑ (2↑) (2↑) 2↗ 2↗ 1↓ (1↓) 1↗ 1↓

A5   G5

ev - 'ry - bod - y knows that smok - in' ain't al - lowed in

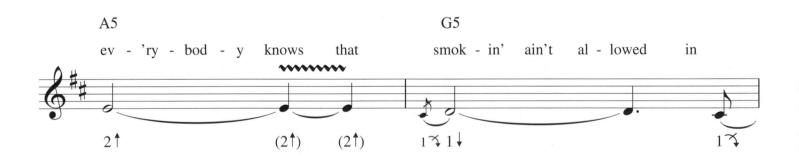

2↑ (2↑) (2↑) 1↗ 1↓ 1↗

D5

school.   *Spoken: Hey, can I be excused?*

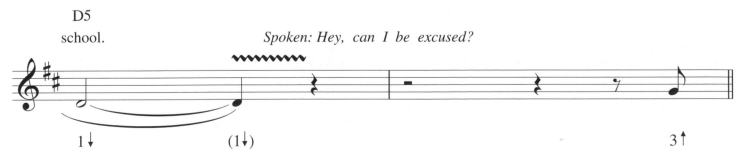

1↓ (1↓) 3↑

Harmonica Solo

Guitar Solo

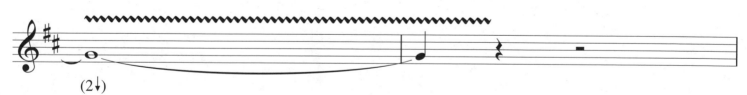

D.S. al Coda 2

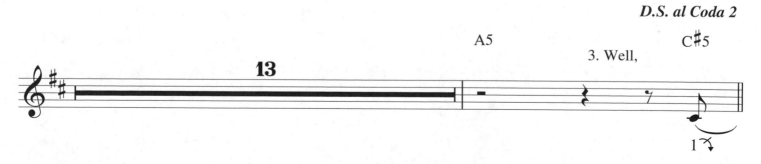

Coda 2

Chorus

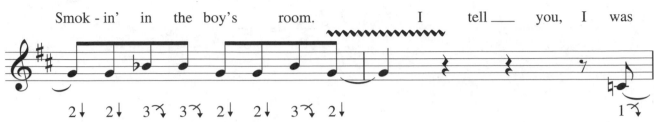

G5

Smok - in' in the boy's room. I tell ___ you, I was

2↓ 2↓ 3↷ 3↷ 2↓ 2↓ 3↷ 2↓ 1↷

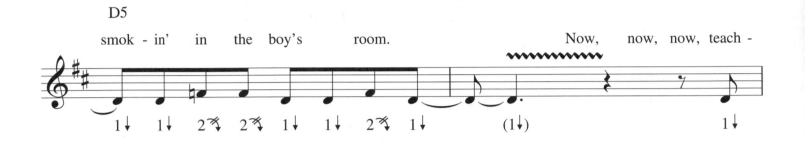

D5

smok - in' in the boy's room. Now, now, now, teach -

1↓ 1↓ 2↷ 2↷ 1↓ 1↓ 2↷ 1↓ (1↓) 1↓

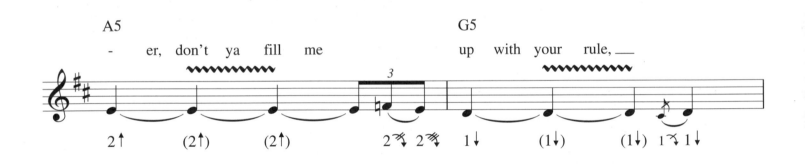

A5   G5

- er, don't ya fill me up with your rule, ___

2↑ (2↑) (2↑) 2↷ 2↷ 1↓ (1↓) (1↓) 1↷ 1↓

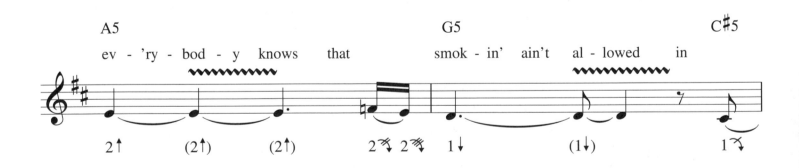

A5   G5   C#5

ev - 'ry - bod - y knows that smok - in' ain't al - lowed in

2↑ (2↑) (2↑) 2↷ 2↷ 1↓ (1↓) 1↷

Outro-Chorus

D5   E5 F5 F#5   N.C.

school.   Ev - 'ry - bod - y.   Smok - in' in the boy's room.

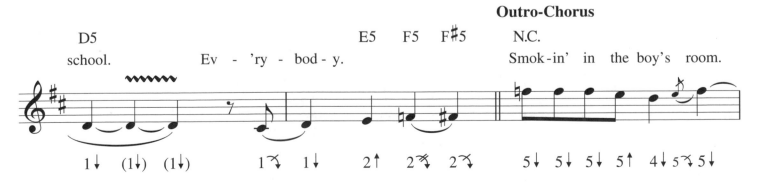

1↓ (1↓) (1↓) 1↷ 1↓ 2↑ 2↷ 2↷ 5↓ 5↓ 5↓ 5↑ 4↓ 5↷ 5↓

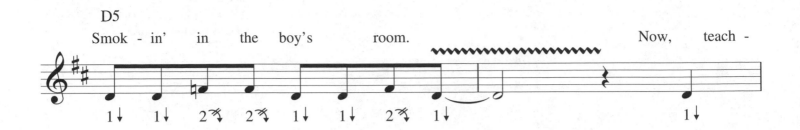

D5 | Smok - in' in the boy's room. | Now, teach -

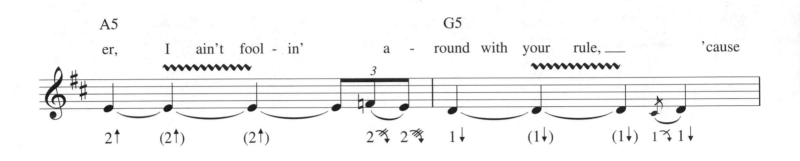

A5   G5

er, I ain't fool - in' a - round with your rule, ___ 'cause

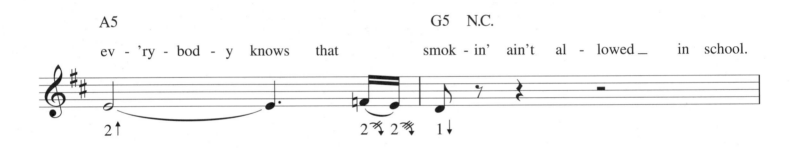

A5   G5 N.C.

ev - 'ry - bod - y knows that smok - in' ain't al - lowed ___ in school.

D9 N.C.

rit.

Additional Lyrics

2. Checkin' out the hall, makin' sure the coast is clear.
   Lookin' in the stalls. Nah, there ain't nobody here.
   My buddies, Sixx, Mick and Tom,
   To get caught would surely be the death of us all.

3. Well, put me to work in the school bookstore
   Checkout counter, and I got bored.
   Teacher was lookin' for me all around.
   Two hours later, you know where I was found.

Train in Vain

Words and Music by Mick Jones and Joe Strummer

HARMONICA
Player: Bob Jones
Harp Key: A Diatonic

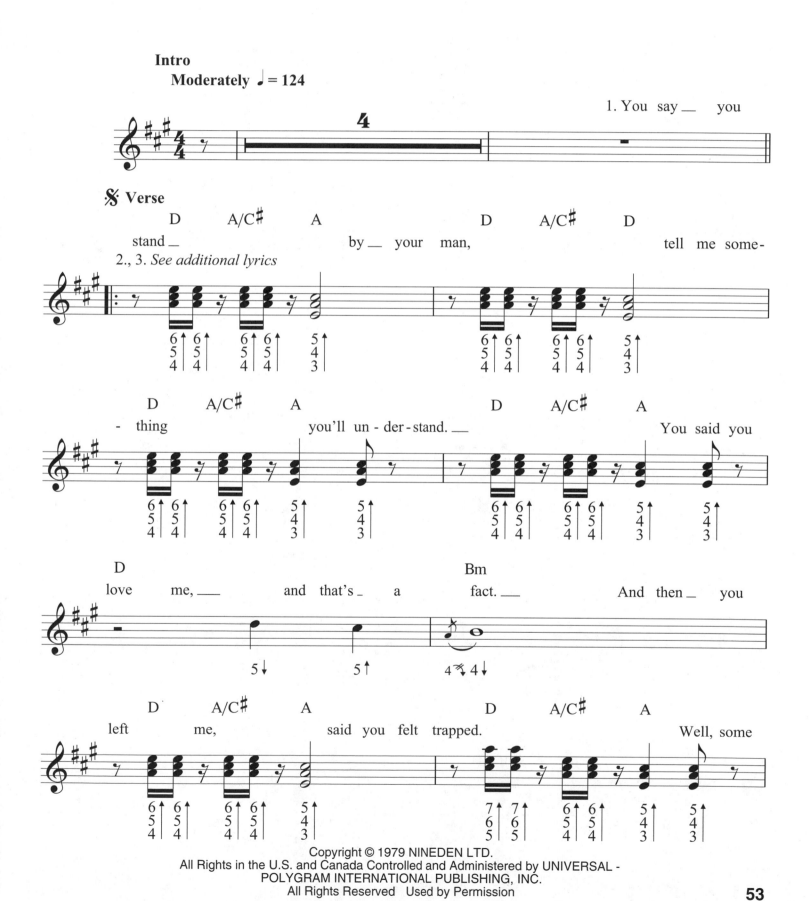

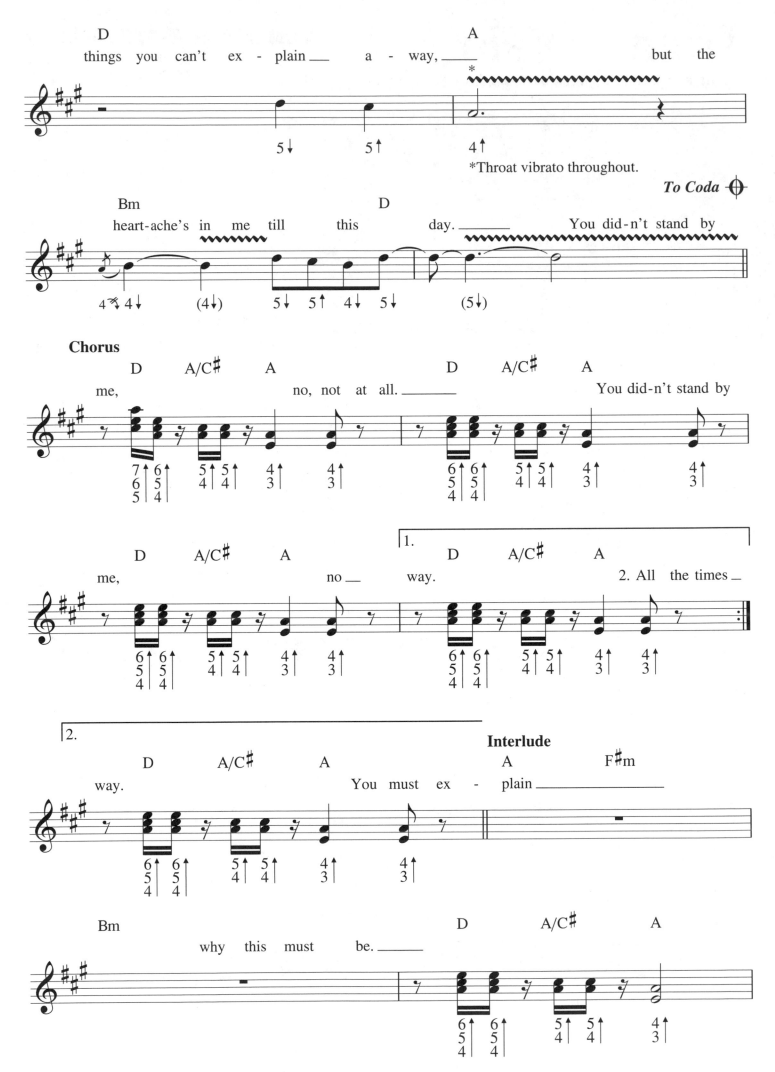

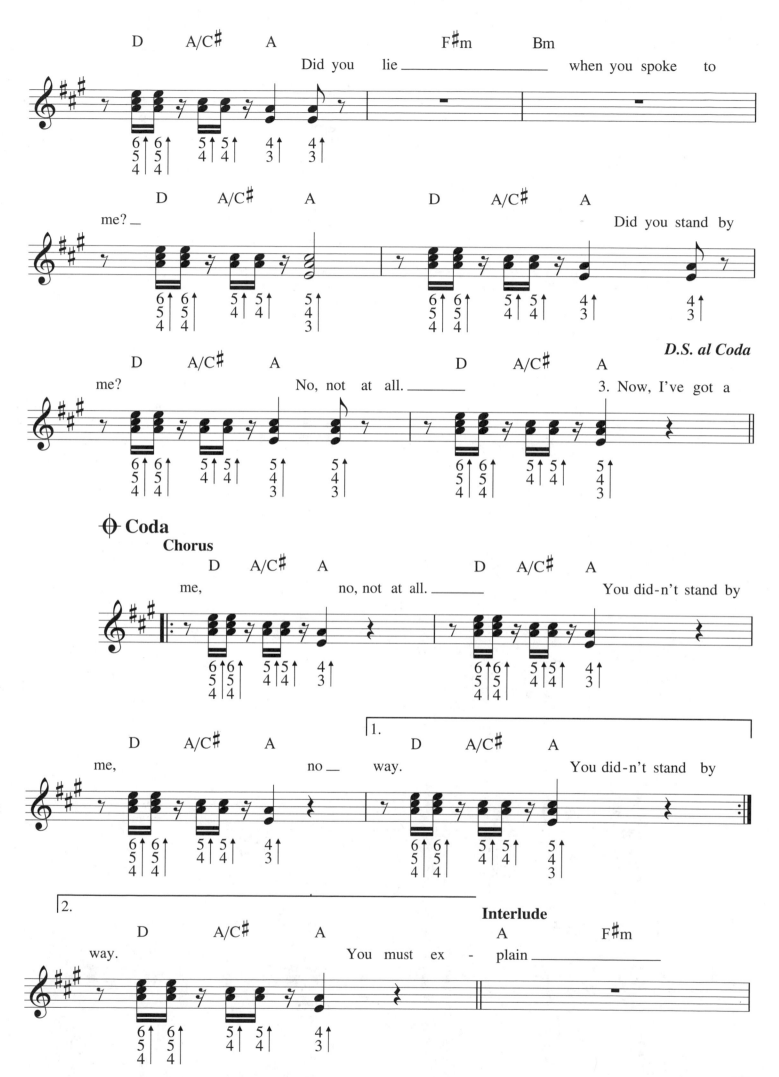

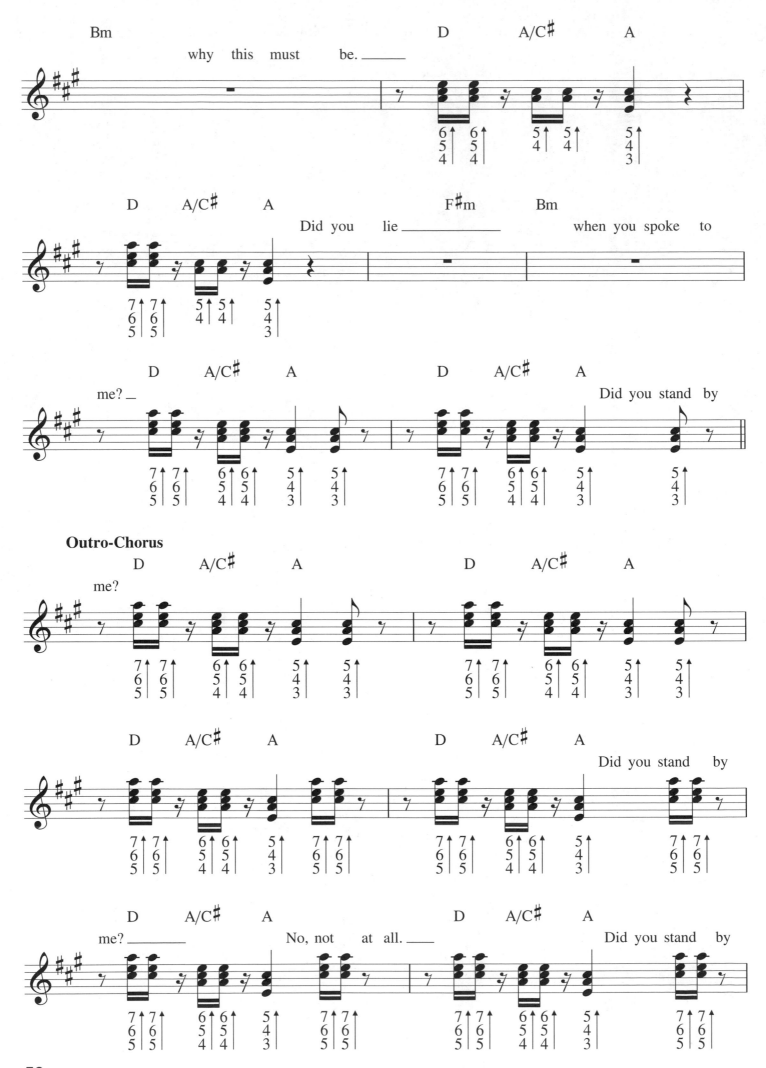

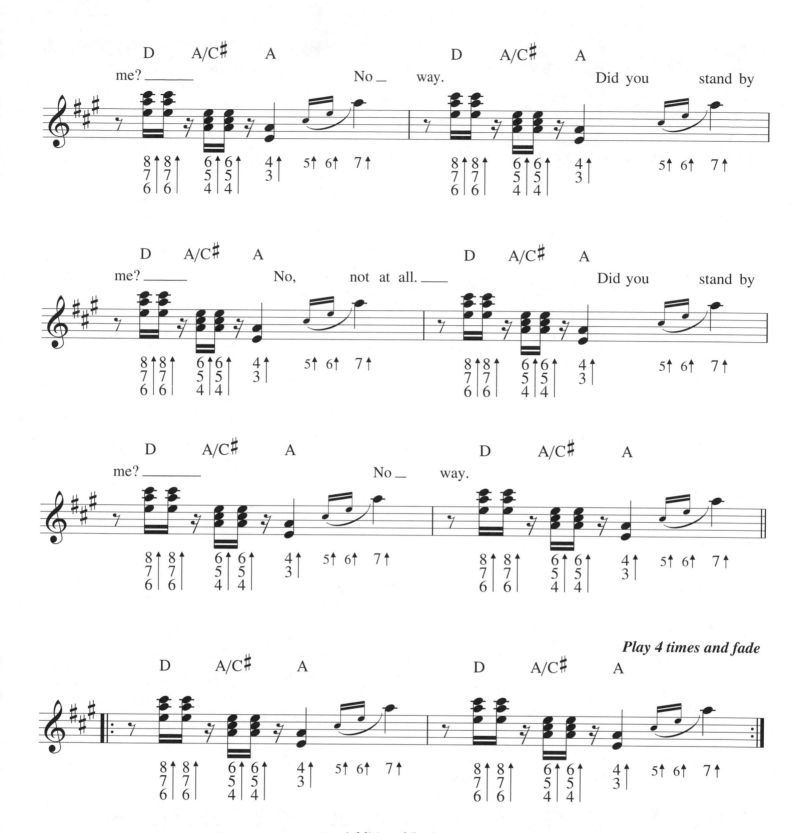

Additional Lyrics

2. All the times when we were close,
   I'll remember these things the most.
   I've seen all my dreams come tumbling down.
   I'm gonna be happy without you around.
   So, alone I'll keep the wolves at bay,
   And there's only one thing I can say.

3. Now, I've got a job, but it don't pay.
   I need new clothes, I need someone to save.
   But without all of these things I can do,
   But without your love, I won't make it through.
   But you don't understand my point of view,
   I suppose there's nothing I can do.

What I Like About You

Words and Music by Michael Skill, Wally Palamarchuk and James Marinos

HARMONICA
Player: Wally Palmar
Harp Key: A Diatonic

Guitar Solo

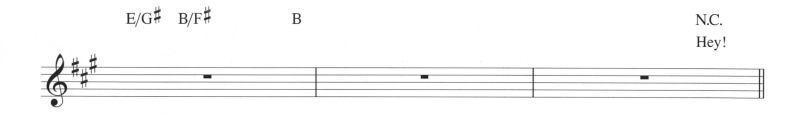

Harmonica Solo

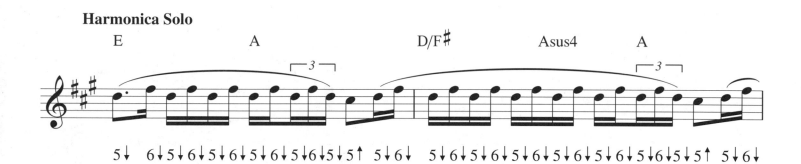

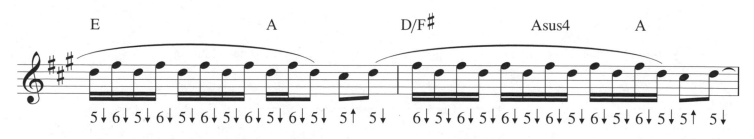

The Harmonica Play-Along Series

Play your favorite songs quickly and easily!

Just follow the notation, listen to the CD to hear how the harmonica should sound, and then play along using the separate backing tracks. The melody and lyrics are also included in the book in case you want to sing, or to simply help you follow along. The audio CD is playable on any CD player. For PC and MAC computer users, the CD is enhanced so you can adjust the recording to any tempo without changing pitch!

1. Pop/Rock
And When I Die • Bright Side of the Road • I Should Have Known Better • Low Rider • Miss You • Piano Man • Take the Long Way Home • You Don't Know How It Feels.
00000478..$12.99

2. Rock Hits
Cowboy • Hand in My Pocket • Karma Chameleon • Middle of the Road • Run Around • Smokin' in the Boys Room • Train in Vain • What I like About You.
00000479..$12.99

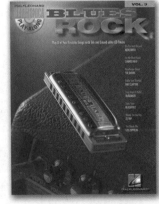

3. Blues/Rock
Big Ten Inch Record • On the Road Again • Roadhouse Blues • Rollin' and Tumblin' • Train Kept A-Rollin' • Train, Train • Waitin' for the Bus • You Shook Me.
00000481..$12.99

Prices, content, and availability subject to change without notice.

HAL•LEONARD®
CORPORATION
7777 W. BLUEMOUND RD. P.O. BOX 13819
MILWAUKEE, WISCONSIN 53213

www.halleonard.com

1108